RESOURCE ROOM
CHURCH HOUSE
9 THE CLOSE
WINCHESTER
SO23 9LS
Tel: 01962 844644

WINCHESTER SCHOOL OF MISSION

D1145314

Words of

Comfort

In loving memory of

Hilda Lucy Dibbin

Words of

Comfort

compiled by
Christopher Herbert

National Society/Church House Publishing

National Society/Church House Publishing,
Church House,
Great Smith Street,
London
SW1P 3NZ

ISBN 0 7151 4851 6

First published in 1994 by The National Society and
Church House Publishing

Introduction and compilation © 1994 Christopher
Herbert

No part of this publication may be reproduced or
transmitted in any form or by any means, electronic or
mechanical, including photocopy, or stored in any
information storage and retrieval system, without
permission in writing from the publisher.

Cover design and illustration by Julian Smith

Text design and typesetting by The National Society

Printed in India by Indeprint Print Production Services

CONTENTS

Other books available in this series:

Pocket Prayers
compiled by Christopher Herbert

Pocket Graces
compiled by Pam Robertson

Introduction

When we are in great sorrow or have been bereaved, after the initial shock and numbness have worn off we try to make sense of what has happened. To do so we turn to family and friends, to neighbours, to clergy, doctors and counsellors, but the ones who can usually give the most help are those who have been in the same situation as ourselves and have come through it.

This collection of writings is just that: the insights, hopes, fears and joys of our fellow human beings who themselves have walked through the valley of the shadow. Some of the pieces are full of hope and serenity, others of bewilderment and anger. I have included these latter because to know that other people have feelings similar to our own can be a real strength and a hidden blessing.

Behind all the writings, however, lies the possibility of God. It is the Christian belief that no matter what the world can throw at us, God will always be there sharing the trial and staying with us until, through grace, we are born anew into eternity.

Christopher Herbert

The Lord is my shepherd: therefore can I lack nothing.

He shall feed me in a green pasture: and lead me forth beside the waters of comfort.

He shall convert my soul: and bring me forth in the paths of righteousness, for his Name's sake.

Yea, though I walk through the valley of the shadow of death, I will fear no evil: for thou art with me; thy rod and thy staff comfort me.

Thou shalt prepare a table before me against them that trouble me: thou hast anointed my head with oil, and my cup shall be full.

But thy loving-kindness and mercy shall follow me all the days of my life: and I will dwell in the house of the Lord for ever.

Psalm 23

When Jesus saw the crowds, he went up the mountain; and after he sat down, his disciples came to him. Then he began to speak, and taught them, saying:

'Blessed are the poor in spirit, for theirs is the kingdom of heaven.
'Blessed are those who mourn, for they will be comforted.
'Blessed are the meek, for they will inherit the earth.
'Blessed are those who hunger and thirst for righteousness, for they will be filled.
'Blessed are the merciful, for they will receive mercy.
'Blessed are the pure in heart, for they will see God.
'Blessed are the peacemakers, for they will be called children of God.
'Blessed are those who are persecuted for righteousness' sake, for theirs is the kingdom of heaven.'

Matthew 5: 1-9

He will feed his flock like a shepherd;
he will gather the lambs in his arms,
and carry them in his bosom,
and gently lead the mother sheep.

Isaiah 40: 11

What is Dying?

For God so loved the world that he gave his only Son, so that everyone who believes in him may not perish but have eternal life.

John 3: 16

What is dying?

*D*ying is the place where our human frailty is most exposed. We are no longer in control of events. Events, this time in our own bodies, are in control of us. We may approach this moment in our own lives full of faith or perhaps with no faith at all.

For the Christian, however, death as well as everything else is held within the power of God, and, in a sense, neither faith nor faithlessness matter, all that matters is the boundless grace of God. Death is not beyond God's reach, it is not outside his love, it is simply the gateway to a new creation, the beginning of life everlasting, the means by which we are taken closer to his heart.

What is dying?

What is dying? I am standing on the sea shore. A ship sails to the morning breeze and starts for the ocean. She is an object of beauty and I stand watching her till at last she fades on the horizon, and someone at my side says, 'She is gone.' Gone where? Gone from my sight, that is all; she is just as large in the masts, hull and spars as she was when I saw her, and just as able to bear her load of living freight to its destination.

The diminished size and total loss of sight is in me, not in her; and just at the moment when someone at my side says, 'She is gone,' there are others who are watching her coming, and other voices take up a glad shout, 'There she comes' – and that is dying.

Charles Henry Brent (1862-1929)

What is dying? ————————

We can know God in the same way a man can see a limitless ocean when he is standing by the shore with a candle during the night. Do you think he can see very much? Nothing much, scarcely anything. And yet, he can see the water well, he knows that in front of him is the ocean and that this ocean is enormous and that he cannot contain it all in his gaze. So it is with our knowledge of God.

St Symeon the New Theologian

Love's constancy

Anyone who has waded
Through Love's turbulent waters,
Now feeling hunger and now satiety,
Is untouched by the seasons
Of withering or blooming,
For in the deepest
And most dangerous waters,
On the highest peaks,
Love is always the same.

Hadewijch of Brabant

What is dying? ────────

Walking away

It is eighteen years ago, almost to the day –
A sunny day with the leaves just turning,
The touch-lines new-ruled – since I watched you play
Your first game of football, then, like a satellite
Wrenched from its orbit, go drifting away

Behind a scatter of boys. I can see
You walking away from me towards the school
With the pathos of a half-fledged thing set free
Into the wilderness, the gait of one
Who finds no path where the path should be.

That hesitant figure, eddying away
Like a winged seed loosened from its parent stem,
Has something I never quite grasp to convey
About nature's give-and-take – the small, the scorching
Ordeals which fire one's irresolute clay.

I have had worse partings, but none that so
Gnaws at my mind still. Perhaps it is roughly
Saying what God alone could perfectly show –
How selfhood begins with walking away,
And love is proved in the letting go.

C Day Lewis

What is dying?

Alone with none but thee, my God,
I journey on my way.
What need I fear, when thou art near
O king of night and day?
More safe am I within thy hand
Than if a host did round me stand.

St Columba (521-597)

As you love me,
Let there be no mourning when I go
Rather of your sweet courtesy
Rejoice with me
At my soul's loosing from captivity

Anon

What is dying? ————————————

L ove is the synthesis of contemplation and
action, the meeting point between heaven and
earth, between God and man.

I have known the satisfaction of unrestrained
action, and the joy of the contemplative life in the
dazzling peace of the desert, and I repeat again St
Augustine's words: 'Love and do as you will.'
Don't worry about what you ought to do. Worry
about loving. Don't interrogate heaven repeatedly
and uselessly saying, 'What course of action
should I pursue?' Concentrate on loving instead.

And by loving you will find out what is for you.
Loving, you will listen to the Voice. Loving, you
will find peace.

Love is the fulfilment of the law and should be
everyone's rule of life; in the end it's the solution
to every problem, the motive for all good.

Carlo Carretto

In the midst of life

Death and I are only nodding acquaintances
We have not been formally introduced
But many times I have noticed
The final encounter
Here in this hospice,
I can truly say
That death has been met with dignity.
Who can divine the thoughts
Of a man in close confrontation?
I can only remember
One particular passing
When a man,
With sustained smile,
Pointed out what was for him
Evidently a great light.
Who knows what final revelations
Are received in the last hours?
Lord, grant me a star in the East
As well as a smouldering sunset.

Sidney G Reeman (d.1975)

What is dying?

O my God, I have no idea where I am going. I do not see the road ahead of me . . . Nor do I really know myself, and the fact that I think I am following your will does not mean that I am actually doing so. But I desire to do your will, and know that the very desire pleases you. Therefore, I will trust you always though I may seem to be lost. I will not fear, for you are always with me, O my dear God.

Thomas Merton (1915-1968)

G rant, O Lord, to all those who are bearing pain, thy spirit of healing, thy spirit of life, thy spirit of peace and hope, of courage and endurance. Cast out from them the spirit of anxiety and fear; grant them perfect confidence and trust in thee, that in thy light they may see light; through Jesus Christ our Lord.

Anon

What is dying?

Watch thou, O Lord, with those who wake, or watch, or weep tonight, and give thine angels charge over those who sleep. Tend thy sick ones, O Lord Christ; rest thy weary ones; bless thy dying ones; soothe thy suffering ones; pity thine afflicted ones; shield thy joyous ones, and all for thy love's sake.

St Augustine (354-430)

What is dying?

I will lift up mine eyes unto the hills from whence cometh my help.

My help cometh from the Lord: who hath made heaven and earth. He will not suffer thy foot to be moved: and he that keepeth thee will not sleep. Behold, he that keepeth Israel: shall neither slumber nor sleep.

The Lord himself is thy keeper: the Lord is thy defence upon thy right hand;

So that the sun shall not burn thee by day: neither the moon by night.

The Lord shall preserve thee from all evil: yea, it is even he that shall keep thy soul.

The Lord shall preserve thy going out, and thy coming in: from this time forth for evermore.

Psalm 121

God be in my head,
And in my understanding;

God be in my eyes,
And in my looking;

God be in my mouth,
And in my speaking;

God be in my heart,
And in my thinking;

God be at my end,
And at my departing.

Pynson's Horae

What is dying? ——————

I rest on God, who will assuredly not allow me to find the meaning of life in his love and forgiveness, to be wholly dependent upon him for the gift of myself, and then to destroy that meaning, revoke that gift. He who holds me in existence now, can and will hold me in it still, through and beyond the dissolution of my mortal frame. For this is the essence of love, to affirm the right of the beloved to exist. And what God affirms, nothing and no one can contradict.

John Austin Baker

Confusion, Anger, Joy and Courage

For I am convinced that neither death, nor life, nor angels, nor rulers, nor things present, nor things to come, nor powers, nor height, nor depth, nor anything else in all creation, will be able to separate us from the love of God in Christ Jesus our Lord.

Romans 8: 38-39

A nd when it comes to our feelings, those who have been left behind, discover a vast ocean. Sometimes the ocean seems calm and still, and yet the next minute, for no apparent reason, a wave comes crashing over us. At other times the loss is so intense it is like being at sea, out of the sight of land and simply tossed around; and then, sometimes there are moments of quiet and serene beauty as a new truth dawns, and sometimes the grief is so overwhelming that it's like drowning, and there's no-one to hear our cries.

*In Jesus' own life there were similar experiences –
of intense and profound closeness to God and of
intense and lonely anguish ('My God, my God,
why hast thou forsaken me?') If God was in Christ
tnen we can believe, without delusion, that
whatever our feelings may be, God is with us,
calming the storm, bringing us peace.*

— *Confusion, anger, joy and courage*

Lord, on your cross you consecrate bodily
weakness to the work of salvation.
Disease, infirmity, hunger and thirst,
you have made them yours:
They are your servants, the messengers
who do your bidding;
Adored in strength, now I worship you in
weakness,
yours and mine.

John Mason Neale (1818-1866)

Confusion, anger, joy and courage ——

O Lord Jesus,
 Please abide with me.
Dispel my deep loneliness!
No one can be my companion for ever
But you are the Lord who is everywhere
Present at all times
Only you are my dear companion and saviour.

In the long dark night
Along the silent shadowy pathways
I beg you to grasp my hand.
When others have forgotten me
Please remember me in eternity!
In the name of Jesus. Amen.

Dr Andrew Song

— *Confusion, anger, joy and coura*

L ord, all these years we were so close to one another, we did everything together, we seemed to know what each was feeling, without the need of words, and now she is gone. Every memory hurts . . . sometimes there comes a feeling that she is near, just out of sight. Sometimes I feel your reproach that to be so submerged in grief is not to notice that she is as eager to keep in touch with me, as I with her. O dear Lord, I pray out of a sore heart that it may b so, daring to believe that it can be so.

George Appleton (1902-1993)

Confusion, anger, joy and courage ———

The prayer of simply being oneself

No one is nearer to God than the man who has a hunger, a want – however tiny and inarticulate. And that is where prayer can begin, the prayer of simply being oneself in utter sincerity.

One can pray like this: 'O my God, I want thee, help me to want thee more.' 'O my God, I love thee so little, help me to love thee as thou lovest me.' 'O my God, I scarcely believe in thee, increase my tiny faith.' 'O my God, I do not really feel sorry for my sin: but I want to, give me a true sorrow for it.'

We don't find God by trying to be more religious than we are or can be.

No, we are near God by being true to ourselves, and then God can begin to find us, to fill our emptiness, and some of the old phrases of religion can be near to what is in the heart.

Michael Ramsey

— *Confusion, anger, joy and courage*

Death, be not proud, though some have called thee
 Mighty and dreadful; for thou art not so.
For those whom thou think'st thou dost overthrow
Die not, poor Death, nor yet can'st thou kill me.
From rest and sleep, which but thy pictures be,
Much pleasure, then from thee much more must flow;
And soonest our best men with thee do go –
Rest of their bones, and soul's delivery.

Thou art slave to Fate, chance, kings and desperate men,
And dost with poison, war, and sickness dwell;
And poppy or charms can make us sleep as well
And better then thy stroke; why swellst thou then?

One short sleep past, we wake eternally
And death shall be no more; Death, thou shalt die.

John Donne (1571-1631)

— *Confusion, anger, joy and courage*

There is no timetable for the human heart: its woes and joys do not work by any clock or calendar. Indeed, I doubt if most of us who have lost one we love could pinpoint an actual moment, day, week or month when we knew that our grief was done. Grief must not, cannot be hurried. If we are wise, we shall not strive to be cured nor keep taking a look within to see how we are getting on. We shall look outward and forward rather than back and discover that we can take the sudden heartache and searing memories in our stride as we gently welcome new activities, opportunities, friendships and interests. We have gained new strength as we have learnt to accept our loss.

Elizabeth Collick

Confusion, anger, joy and courage ———

'You will not be overcome'

Our Lord spoke these words with utter certainty:
'You will not be overcome.'

And this teaching and true comfort are for all my
fellow Christians . . .

The words, 'You will not be overcome' were
spoken firmly to give assurance and comfort
against all the troubles that might come.

He did not say, 'You will not be tempested, you
will not be troubled, you will not be distressed.'

He said, 'You will not be overcome.'

It is God's will that we pay attention to His words
and that we remain strong in certainty in
prosperity and trouble. Because he loves us he
wants us to love him and trust him – and all shall
be well.

Julian of Norwich (1342-1413)

— *Confusion, anger, joy and courage*

L et nothing disturb thee,
 Let nothing dismay thee:
All things pass:
God never changes.
Patience attains
All that it strives for:
He who has God
Finds he lacks nothing:
God alone suffices.

St Teresa of Avila (1515-1582)

— *Confusion, anger, joy and courage*

He is with me when I am alone

In the time of joy I might have said with Paul, 'Nothing shall separate me from the love of Christ.' And in pain I might have said with St Peter, 'Lord, save me. I perish.'

This was revealed to teach me that it is necessary for everyone to experience this – sometimes to have comfort, and sometimes to fail and be left alone.

Sometimes for the profit of his soul, a man is left to himself, and not because he has sinned.

God wants us to know that he upholds us eternally secure in prosperity and adversity, and loves us as much in times of trouble as when we prosper.

It is God's will that we hold fast to his comfort with all our might, because joy is everlasting and suffering passes and will be brought to nothing.

Julian of Norwich (1342-1413)

Confusion, anger, joy and courage ——

L ead, kindly Light, amid the encircling gloom,
  Lead thou me on;
The night is dark, and I am far from home;
Lead thou me on.
Keep thou my feet; I do not ask to see
The distant scene; one step enough for me.

I was not ever thus, nor prayed that thou
Shouldst lead me on;
I loved to choose and see my path; but now
Lead thou me on.
I loved the garish day, and, spite of fears,
Pride ruled my will: remember not past years.

So long thy power hath blest me, sure it still
Will lead me on,
O'er moor and fen, o'er crag and torrent, till
The night is gone,
And with the morn those angel faces smile,
Which I have loved long since, and lost awhile.

John Henry Newman (1801-1890)

— *Confusion, anger, joy and courage*

I am not alone

I am alone but not alone, and I am grateful.
Not only are you with me, God, but so, in
spirit, are all that great company of people
who try to follow you.

Even living near me there are people I don't
know who love you as I love you. Every time
I try and fail and am forgiven and try again, I
feel the unseen companionship of many other people.

You have a family, God, a family millions
strong and yet still close. It gives me strength
and comfort to remember this, and I thank you.

Avery Brooke

Confusion, anger, joy and courage —

I pray that the true God may protect me tonight
Keep me safe from turmoil and trouble.
I pray also for my family and friends,
For all people all over the world –

I pray the cloud of your compassion
May cover them and grant them peace.

Dr F Y Zia

Via Dolorosa

Do not make the mistake
of imagining that you
may go singing
on the Via Dolorosa
neither may you
bear right or left
the way is confined
with little room
for manoeuvre

You will know exhaustion
kneeling often
trodden and rough
and scarred by many feet
this way is our way
and may not be shunned
turned from
or avoided
best to go quietly
with a dogged courage
knowing that
one thing is certain:
There is an end

Confusion, anger, joy and courage ——

And when you arrive
you will find
that the hill is crowned
with a living tree
stretching out
great branches
to give you shelter
and manna there
and spring water

Margaret Torrie

No one shall be able to stand against you all
the days of your life. As I was with Moses,
so I will be with you; I will not fail you or forsake
you.

Joshua 1: 5

— *Confusion, anger, joy and courage*

Do not let your hearts be troubled. Believe in God, believe also in me. In my Father's house there are many dwelling places. If it were not so, would I have told you that I go to prepare a place for you? And if I go and prepare a place for you, I will come again and I will take you to myself, so that where I am, there you may be also. And you know the way to the place where I am going.' Thomas said to him, 'Lord, we do not know where you are going. How can we know the way?' Jesus said to him, 'I am the way, and the truth, and the life. No one comes to the Father except through me.'

John 14: 1-6

Confusion, anger, joy and courage ——

The existence of love

I had thought that your death
  Was a waste and a destruction,
A pain of grief hardly to be endured.
I am only beginning to learn
That your life was a gift and a growing
And a loving left with me.
The desperation of death
Destroyed the existence of love,
But the fact of death
Cannot destroy what has been given.
I am learning to look at your life again
Instead of your death and your departing.

Marjorie Pizer

The Funeral

B lessed are those who mourn, for they shall be comforted.

Matthew 5: 4

The funeral

*When I was a parish priest it was my great
privilege to conduct funerals. Even in the
most tragic and poignant circumstance I rejoiced
in the opening sentence of the service: 'I am the
Resurrection and the life, saith the Lord . . .' It
was a resounding acclamation of belief, a
statement that Christ had conquered death.*

*Inevitably before a funeral there is often much
apprehension, bewilderment, fear – especially the
fear of somehow breaking down. But I was always
struck, even at times when there was extreme
sorrow, by the nobility and dignity of human
beings; by their humble bravery. And I was always
glad to end the service with that great blessing:
'Go into the world in peace; be of good courage;
hold fast to that which is good, render to no man
evil for evil, strengthen the faint-hearted, support
the weak; help the afflicted; honour all men, love
and serve the Lord rejoicing in the power of the
Holy Spirit and the blessing . . .'*

O Father of all, we pray to thee for those whom we love, but see no longer. Let light perpetual shine upon them; and in thy loving wisdom and almighty power work in them the good purpose of thy perfect will; through Jesus Christ our Lord. Amen.

Book of Common Prayer (1928)

A lmighty God, Father of all mercies and giver of all comfort: deal graciously, we pray, with those who mourn, that casting all their care on you, they may know the consolation of your love; through Jesus Christ our Lord. Amen.

Alternative Service Book 1980

The funeral

O Lord, support us all the day long of this troublous life, until the shades lengthen, the evening comes, the busy world is hushed, the fever of life is over, and our work is done. Then, Lord, in your mercy grant us safe lodging, a holy rest, and peace, at the last, through Jesus Christ our Lord. Amen.

John Henry Newman (1801-1890)

F ather in heaven, you gave your Son Jesus Christ to suffering and to death on the cross, and raised him to life in glory. Grant us a patient faith in time of darkness, and strengthen our hearts with the knowledge of your love; through Jesus Christ our Lord. Amen.

Alternative Service Book 1980

At a funeral

Eternal Lord God, grant me a glimpse into the new order of being into which your child has now entered; may he feel at home there and continue to grow in happiness, holiness, maturity and love. I thank you that our relationships of love cannot be broken by physical death. I cannot but be sad that he is out of physical sight, yet not out of touch, for we are both in your hands and nothing harmful can hurt us. Unto your gracious mercy and protection we commit him. May he see the smile of your welcome and smile back in warm gratitude and love, O Father of souls.

George Appleton (1902-1993)

The funeral

B e thou a bright flame before me,
Be thou a guiding star above me,
Be thou a smooth path below me,
Be thou a kindly shepherd behind me,
Today, tonight and for ever.

St Columba (521-597)

E ven he whom we call dead is alive this day.

In the presence of God
we lay him down;
in the power of God
he shall rise;
in the person of Christ
he is risen already.

John Donne (1571-1631)

Go forth upon thy journey from this world, O Christian soul
 in the peace of him in whom thou hast believed,
 in the name of God the Father, who created thee,
 in the name of Jesus Christ who suffered for thee,
 in the name of the Holy Spirit, who strengthened thee.
May angels and archangels, and all the armies of the heavenly host, come to meet thee,
may all the saints of God welcome thee,
may thy portion this day be in gladness and peace, thy dwelling in Paradise,
Go forth upon thy journey, O Christian Soul.

Prayer for the dying, from the Roman Ritual

The funeral

Christ is the morning star who
  when the darkness of the world is past
brings to his saints
the promise of the light of life
and opens everlasting day.

Venerable Bede (673-735)

If I should go before the rest of you,
  Break not a flower nor inscribe a stone.
Nor when I'm gone speak in a Sunday voice,
But be the usual selves that I have known.
Weep if you must,
Parting is hell,
But life goes on,
So sing as well.

Joyce Grenfell

Remember

Remember me when I am gone away,
Gone far away into the silent land;
When you can no more hold me by the hand,
Nor I half turn to go yet turning stay.
Remember me when no more day by day
You tell me of our future that you'd plann'd:
Only remember me; you understand
It will be late to counsel then or pray.
Yet if you should forget me for a while
And afterwards remember, do not grieve:
For if the darkness and corruption leave
A vestige of the thoughts that once I had,
Better by far that you should forget and smile
Than that you should remember and be sad.

Christina Rossetti (1830-1894)

The funeral

It is never the beginning of the story to say a child is born, nor is it the end to say a man has died, for long preparation leads up to every birth, and a death leaves behind it a power for good or evil that works on in the world for longer than the span of life from which it grew. In the case of those whom we call the saints this power is immeasurable. They are the true makers of men. Other great men may alter the material aspect of life for millions but the saints make us for eternity.

Elizabeth Goudge

Listen, I will tell you a mystery! We will not all die, but we will all be changed, in a moment, in the twinkling of an eye, at the last trumpet. For the trumpet will sound and the dead will be raised imperishable, and we will be changed. For this perishable body must put on imperishability, and this mortal body must put on immortality. When this perishable body puts on imperishability, and this mortal body puts on immortality, then the saying that is written will be fulfilled:

  'Death has been swallowed up in victory.'
  'Where, O death, is your victory?
  Where, O death, is your sting?'

The sting of death is sin, and the power of sin is the law. But thanks be to God, who gives us the victory through our Lord Jesus Christ.

1 Corinthians 15: 51-57

The funeral

We cannot arrive at the perfect possession of God in this life, and that is why we are travelling and in darkness. But we already possess him by grace, and therefore in that sense we have arrived and are dwelling in the light.

But oh! How far have I to go to find you in whom I have already arrived!

For now, O my God, it is to you alone that I can talk, because nobody else will understand. I cannot bring any other man on this earth into the cloud where I dwell in your light, that is, your darkness, where I am lost and abashed. I cannot explain to any other man the anguish which is your joy nor the loss which is the possession of you, nor the distance from all things which is the arrival in you, nor the death which is the birth in you because I do not know anything about myself and all I know is that I wish it were over – I wish it were begun.

Thomas Merton (1915-1968)

Journey Towards God

For the Lamb at the centre of the throne will be their shepherd, and he will guide them to springs of the water of life, and God will wipe away every tear from their eyes.

Revelation 7: 17

Journey towards God

It would be a folly to imagine that once the funeral is over life can get back to normal again. It is not as simple as that. The feelings continue to dance their own dance, often outside our own control. There are new patterns of living to be discovered, decisions to be made, a new kind of life to be lived. And we may also become aware in a sharp and painful way of our own mortality.

For many of us the image of life as a journey is helpful; especially if we believe that the destiny of that journey is God; so that although there may be much pain and loss, we can with courage trust that we are not alone and that Christ is the hidden companion who walks with us every step of the way.

Journey towards God

Death is nothing at all . . . I have only slipped away into the next room. I am I and you are you. Whatever we were to each other that we are still. Call me by my old familiar name, speak to me in the easy way which you always used. Put no difference in your tone; wear no forced air of solemnity or sorrow. Laugh as we always laughed at the little jokes we enjoyed together. Play, smile, think of me, pray for me. Let my name be ever the household word that it always was. Let it be spoken without effort, without the ghost of a shadow on it. Life means all that it ever meant. It is the same as it ever was: there is absolutely unbroken continuity. Why should I be out of mind because I am out of sight? I am waiting for you for an interval, somewhere very near, just around the corner. All is well.

Henry Scott Holland (1847-1918)

Journey towards God ——————

We seem to give them back to you, O God, who gave them to us . . . Yet as you did not lose them in giving, so we do not lose them by their return. O lover of souls, you do not give as the world gives. What you give you do not take away; for what is yours is ours also if we are yours. And life is eternal and love is immortal; and death is only a horizon; and a horizon is nothing save the limit of our sight. Lift us up, strong son of God, that we may see further; cleanse our eyes that we may see more clearly; draw us closer to yourself that we may know ourselves to be nearer to our loved ones who are with you. And while you prepare a place for them, prepare us also for that happy place, that where you are we may be also for evermore. Amen.

Charles Henry Brent (1862-1929)

Mourning

He is gone; his pain is over and he is gone.
The funeral is over and the family and friends
have left. The letters are answered.
But the emptiness remains.

The emptiness and so much more. I am
angry, God. I am angry at him for dying and
angry at you for letting him die. I am angry
at friends, who have been so kind, because they
are alive and because those they love are alive.

I am angry because I failed him so often. I
hurt him. I was selfish, thoughtless, mean.
And now he is gone, and I cannot undo the past.

It might be easier to pretend I am not angry
but I cannot fool you, God. Help me through
this time of anger and pain, of guilt and loss.
Help me to live as he – and you – would like
me to live.

Avery Brooke

Journey towards God

G od of the sealed tomb,
   we cannot bear to leave
your dead and buried body.
But you send us away
to mark the long night
of our mourning without you.
You lie in death alone,
beyond the bounds of our feeble knowing.

Numbed by our grief and sorrow,
we cannot interpret you:
you have gone far from us,
down into darkness,
deep into death.

In your great love,
wait for us
where we grieve in the darkness,
till we return to the grave
to find you,
risen, released in the night.

Nicola Slee

———— *Journey towards God*

If the Great Father Creator is as great as death,
surely as creator of the universe, of darkness
and light,
he must be at least equal to his creation;
and in so being,
as an artist is greater than his canvas,
so is he greater than death.

Giles Harcourt

Father of all, by whose mercy and grace your
saints remain in everlasting light and peace:
we remember with thanksgiving those whom we
love but see no longer; and we pray that in them
your perfect will may be fulfilled; through Jesus
Christ our Lord.

Alternative Service Book 1980

Journey towards God ——————

The faith of Christ teaches more than courage in the face of death. Our attitude to death is transformed. As we come to a more intimate experience of the reality of God, we may enter into the overcoming power and strength of the great words of Christ: I am the resurrection and the life.

Death is swallowed up in victory. For those we love it is no longer a dark place of shadows but an entrance into the fuller light of God. Though we naturally grieve at the withdrawal of loved friends from our physical sight, we may still rejoice in their new freedom. The dead are not lost to us; they are still our friends in the service of the Eternal.

Of Joan Mary Fry to her friends, 1955

Journey towards God

On the day of Good Friday
My true love gave to me
His own self upon a bare tree.

On the Saturday that followed
My true love gave to me
Rest after pain
And his own self upon a bare tree.

On the first day of Easter
My true love gave to me
Life, new life,
Rest after pain
And his own self upon a bare tree.

All the day after Easter
My true love gives to me
Grace for my living,
Joy in my giving,
Comfort in sorrow,
Strength for tomorrow,
Love without end –
His risen light,
Life, new life,
Rest after pain
And his own self upon a bare tree.

Pamela Egan

Journey towards God ——————

S ince I am coming to that holy room
Where with thy choir of saints for evermore
I shall be made thy music, as I come
I tune the instrument here at the door
And what I must do then, think here before.

John Donne (1571-1631)

Journey towards God

It is all grace. It is not even that there is a door which Christ has unbolted, and we, standing outside it, have to stretch out our hand, lift the latch, and walk through. We are already inside. When our Saviour became man and undid the sin of Adam, he did not command the cherubim with the flaming sword to return to heaven so that we could re-enter Eden. He picked up the walls of Eden and carried them to the farthest edge of Ocean, and there set them up so that they now girdle the whole world. All we are asked to do is to open our eyes and recognise where we are. Once we have done that, then we shall look down at ourselves and our filthy bodies and our tattered clothes and we shall say, 'I am not fit to be here, in Paradise'; and we shall ask for baptism to wash us clean, and for the white robe of chrism to clothe us in the righteousness of the Lord. But not in order that we may be saved – simply because this is fitting for those who have been saved.

John Austin Baker

Journey towards God ─────────

Into that house they shall enter
and in that house they shall dwell
where there shall be
 no cloud nor sun
 no darkness nor dazzling
but one equal light;
 no noise or silence
but one equal music;
 no fears or hopes
but one equal possession;
 no foes nor friends
but one equal eternity.

Keep us, Lord,
so awake in the duties of our callings
that we may thus sleep in peace
and wake in thy glory.

John Donne (1571-1631)

A Vision of Heaven

Eye has not seen, nor ear heard, nor the heart of man conceived, what God has prepared for those who love him.

1 Corinthians 2: 9

A vision of heaven

*O*ne of my favourite phrases in the Bible is *that spoken by Mary Magdalene when she first saw the Risen Jesus: 'And she, supposing him to be the gardener . . . '. It is so understated, so amazing that the risen Christ should be mistaken for a jobbing gardener pushing a wheelbarrow . . .*

It is not everyone's vision of heaven, but it is mine, because it does not deny this world, quite the opposite, it takes the things of this world and transforms them into glory, revealing the steadfast holy love which God has for each one of us in Christ.

A vision of heaven

Then I saw a new heaven and a new earth; for
the first heaven and the first earth had passed
away, and the sea was no more. And I saw the
holy city, the new Jerusalem, coming down out of
heaven from God, prepared as a bride adorned for
her husband. And I heard a loud voice from the
throne saying,

> 'See, the home of God is among mortals.
> He will dwell with them as their God;
> they will be his people,
> and God himself will be with them;
> he will wipe every tear from their eyes.
> Death will be no more;
> mourning and crying and pain will be no more,
> for the first things have passed away.'

Revelation 21: 1-4

A vision of heaven

We are in a garden, a strange and lovely garden that contains a crimson butterfly. Do not be too certain you can catch that crimson butterfly no matter how fancy your footwork. But if you stop trying to catch it and just begin to enjoy the garden, it may, for less than a moment touch your hand.

Richard Holloway

In the sky
The song of the skylark
Greets the dawn.
In the fields wet with dew
The scent of the violets
Fills the air.
On such a lovely morning as this
Surely on such a lovely morning as this

Lord Jesus
Came forth
From the tomb.

Misuno Genzo 1984

Now the green blade riseth from the buried
  grain,
wheat that in the dark earth many days has lain;
Love lives again, that with the dead has been:
    Love is come again,
    like wheat that springeth green.

In the grave they laid him, Love whom men had slain,
thinking that never he would wake again,
laid in the earth like grain that sleeps unseen:
    Love is come again,
    like wheat that springeth green.

Forth he came at Easter, like the risen grain,
he that for three days in the grave had lain,
quick from the dead my risen Lord is seen:
    Love is come again,
    like wheat that springeth green.

J M C Crum

A vision of heaven

Early on the first day of the week, while it was still dark, Mary Magdalene came to the tomb and saw that the stone had been removed from the tomb. So she ran and went to Simon Peter and the other disciple, the one whom Jesus loved, and said to them, 'They have taken the Lord out of the tomb, and we do not know where they have laid him.' Then Peter and the other disciple set out and went toward the tomb. The two were running together, but the other disciple outran Peter and reached the tomb first. He bent down to look in and saw the linen wrappings lying there, but he did not go in. Then Simon Peter came, following him, and went into the tomb. He saw the linen wrappings lying there, and the cloth that had been on Jesus' head, not lying with the linen wrappings but rolled up in a place by itself. Then the other disciple, who reached the tomb first, also went in, and he saw and believed; for as yet they did not understand the scripture, that he must rise from the dead. Then the disciples returned to their homes.

John 20: 1-10

A vision of heaven

But Mary stood weeping outside the tomb. As she wept, she bent over to look into the tomb; and she saw two angels in white, sitting where the body of Jesus had been lying, one at the head and the other at the feet. They said to her, 'Woman, why are you weeping?' She said to them, 'They have taken away my lord, and I do not know where they have laid him.' When she had said this, she turned around and saw Jesus standing there, but she did not know that it was Jesus. Jesus said to her, 'Woman, why are you weeping? Whom are you looking for?' Supposing him to be the gardener, she said to him, 'Sir, if you have carried him away, tell me where you have laid him, and I will take him away.' Jesus said to her, 'Mary!' She turned and said to him in Hebrew, 'Rabboni!' (which means Teacher). Jesus said to her, 'Do not hold on to me, because I have not yet ascended to the Father. But go to my brothers and say to them, 'I am ascending to my Father and your Father, to my God and your God.'

John 20: 11-18

A vision of heaven

Christy rising in us

The death and resurrection of Christ draw near
to us and touch us in the sacrament. The
bread is broken – there Christ dies; we receive it
as Christ alive – there is his resurrection. It is the
typical expression of divine power to make
something from nothing. God has made the world
where no world was, and God makes life out of
death. Such is the God with whom we have to do.
We do not come to God for a little help, a little
support to our own good intentions. We come to
him for resurrection. God will not be asked for a
little, he will be asked for all. We reckon ourselves
dead, says St Paul, that we may ask God for a
resurrection, not of ourselves, but of Christ in us.

Austin Farrer

We are tempted to believe that, although the Resurrection may be the climax of the Gospel, there is yet a Gospel that stands upon its own feet and may be understood and appreciated before we pass on to the Resurrection. The first disciples did not find this so. For them the Gospel without the Resurrection was not merely a Gospel without its final chapter: it was not a Gospel at all. Jesus Christ had, it is true, taught and done great things: but he did not allow the disciples to rest in these things. He led them on to paradox, perplexity and darkness; and there he left them. There too they would have remained, had he not been raised from death. But his Resurrection threw its own light backwards upon the death and the ministry that went before; it illuminated the paradoxes and disclosed the unity of his words and deeds. As Scott Holland said: 'In the Resurrection it was not only the Lord who was raised from the dead. His life on earth rose with him; it was lifted up into its real light.'

Michael Ramsey

A vision of heaven

(Christian and Hopeful have come through the river of death.)

Now upon the bank of the river, on the other side, they saw the shining men again, who there waited for them. Wherefore being come out of the river, they saluted them, saying, We are ministering spirits, sent forth to minister for those that shall be heirs of salvation. Thus they went along towards the gate.

Now you must note, that the City stood upon a mighty hill; but the pilgrims went up that hill with ease, because they had these two men to lead them up by the arms; also they had left their mortal garments behind them in the river; for though they went in with them, they came out without them. They therefore went up here with much agility and speed, though the foundation upon which the City was framed was higher than the clouds; they therefore went up through the regions of the air, sweetly talking as they went, being comforted because they had safely got over the river, and had such glorious companions to attend them.

The talk that they had with the shining ones was about the glory of the place: who told them that

the beauty and the glory of it was inexpressible.
There, said they, is the Mount Sion, the heavenly
Jerusalem, the innumerable company of angels,
and the spirits of just men made perfect. You are
going now, said they, to the paradise of God,
wherein you shall see the tree of life, and eat of
the never-fading fruits thereof: and when you
come there you shall have white robes given you,
and your walk and talk shall be every day with the
King, even all the days of eternity. There you shall
not see again such things as you saw when you
were in the lower region upon the earth: to wit,
sorrow, sickness, affliction and death; for the
former things are passed away. The men then
asked, What must we do in the holy place? To
whom it was answered, You must there receive
the comfort of all your toil, and have joy for all
your sorrow; you must reap what you have sown,
even the fruit of all your prayers, and tears, and
sufferings for the King by the way. In that place
you must wear crowns of gold, and enjoy the
perpetual sight and visions of the Holy One; for
there you shall see him as he is. There also you
shall serve him continually.

John Bunyan (1628-88) *The Pilgrim's Progress*

Easter wings

Lord who createst man in wealth and store,
though foolishly he lost the same,
decaying more and more,
till he became
most poor,

with thee
Oh let me rise,
as larks, harmoniously,
and sing this day thy victories:
then shall that fall further the flight in me.

My tender age in sorrow did begin,
and still with sicknesses and shame
thou didst so punish sin
that I became
most thin.

With thee
let me combine,
and feel this day thy victory:
for, if I graft my wing on thine,
affliction shall advance the flight in me.

George Herbert (1593-1632)

A vision of heaven

Love's redeeming work is done;
Fought the fight, the battle won:
Lo, our sun's eclipse is o'er!
Lo, he sets in blood no more.

Vain the stone, the watch, the seal,
Christ has burst the gates of hell;
Death in vain forbids his rise;
Christ has opened paradise.

Lives again our glorious king;
Where, O death, is now thy sting?
Dying once, he all doth save;
Where thy vistory, O grave?

Charles Wesley (1707-1788)

A vision of heaven

Where is heaven? Is it some millions of leagues from us, far beyond the sun and the fixed stars? What have immortal spirits to do with space and place? Who knows, but a heaven-born soul, who is freed from the clog of this vile body, and filled with all the fullness of God, may pass as easily and quickly from one verge of the creation to the other, as our thoughts can change and fly from east to west, from the past to the future? Perhaps, even now, we live in the midst of this glorious assembly; heaven is there where our God and Saviour displays himself; and do not you feel him near you, nearer than any of his visible works? Perhaps there is nothing but this thin partition of flesh and blood between us and those blessed spirits that are before the throne. If our eyes were open, we should see the mountains around us covered with chariots and horses of fire; if our ears were unstopped we should hear the praises of our great Immanuel resounding in the air, as once the shepherds heard. What a comfortable meditation is this to strengthen our weak faith in such a dark declining day as this, when sense would almost persuade us that we are left to serve God alone!

John Newton (1725-1807)

A vision of heaven

When it comes to the trial, the question will not be, who hath preached most, or heard most, or talked most, but who hath loved most?

Richard Baxter (1615-1691)

A vision of heaven

The moment of ecstasy

This life is a period of training, a time of
preparation, during which we learn the art of
loving God and our neighbour, the heart of the
Gospel message, sometimes succeeding,
sometimes failing.

Death is the way which leads us to the vision of
God, the moment when we shall see him as he
really is, and find our total fulfilment in love's
final choice.

The ultimate union with that which is most
lovable, union with God, is the moment of ecstasy,
the unending 'now' of complete happiness. That
vision will draw from us the response of surprise,
wonder and joy which will be forever our prayer
of praise. We are made for that.

Basil Hume

Eden Rock

They are waiting for me somewhere beyond
Eden Rock;
My father, twenty-five, in the same suit
Of Genuine Irish Tweed, his terrier Jack
Still two years old and trembling at his feet.

My mother, twenty-three, in a sprigged dress
Drawn at the waist, ribbon in her straw hat,
Has spread the stiff white cloth over the grass.
Her hair, the colour of wheat, takes on the light.

She pours tea from a Thermos, the milk straight
From an old HP sauce-bottle, a screw
Of paper and a cork; slowly sets out
The same three plates, the tin cups painted blue.

The sky whitens as if lit by three suns.
My mother shades her eyes and looks my way
Over the drifted stream. My father spins
A stone along the water. Leisurely,

They beckon to me from the other bank.
I hear them call, 'See, where the stream-path is!
Crossing is not as hard as you might think.'
I had not thought that it would be like this.

Charles Causley

A vision of heaven

Jesus said to her, 'I am the resurrection and the life. Those who believe in me, even though they die, will live, and everyone who lives and believes in me will never die. Do you believe this?'

John 11: 25-26

God's Aid

God to enfold me,
God to surround me,
God in my speaking,
God in my thinking.

God in my sleeping,
God in my waking,
God in my watching,
God in my hoping.

God in my life,
God in my lips,
God in my soul,
God in my heart.

God in my sufficing,
God in my slumber,
God in mine ever-living soul,
God in mine eternity.

Carmina Gadelica

A vision of heaven

Though I speak with the tongues of men and of angels, and have not charity, I am become as sounding brass, or a tinkling cymbal.

And though I have the gift of prophecy, and understand all mysteries, and all knowledge; and though I have faith, so that I could remove mountains, and have not charity, I am nothing.

And though I bestow all my goods to feed the poor, and though I give my body to be burned, and have not charity, it profiteth me nothing.

Charity suffereth long, and is kind; charity envieth not; charity vaunteth not itself, is not puffed up.

Doth not behave itself unseemly, seeketh not her own, is not easily provoked, thinketh no evil;

Rejoiceth not in iniquity, but rejoiceth in the truth;

Beareth all things, believeth all things, hopeth all things, endureth all things.

Charity never faileth: but whether there be prophecies, they shall fail; whether there be knowledge it shall vanish away.

For we know in part, and we prophesy in part.

But when that which is perfect is come, then that which is in part shall be done away.

When I was a child, I spake as a child, I understood as a child: but when I became a man, I put away childish things.

For now we see through a glass, darkly; but then face to face: now I know in part; but then shall I know even as also I am known.

And now abideth faith, hope, charity, these three; but the greatest of these is charity.

1 Corinthians 13

A vision of heaven

God is everywhere but not everywhere to us. There is but one point in the universe where God communicates with us and that is the centre of our own soul.

St Augustine (d. 604)

We shall rest and we shall see, we shall see and we shall love, we shall love and we shall praise, in the end which is no end.

St Augustine (d. 604)

Index of Authors

Index of First Lines

Lord, all these years we were so close, 29
Lord, on your cross you consecrate bodily weakness, 27
Lord who created man in wealth and store, 78
Love is the synthesis of contemplation and action, 18
Love's redeeming work is done, 79

No one is nearer to God than the man who has a
    hunger, 30
No one shall be able to stand against you, 40
Now the green blade riseth, 71
Now upon the bank of the river, 76

O Father of all, 45
O Lord Jesus, please abide with me, 28
O Lord, support us all the day long, 46
O my God, I have no idea where I am going, 20
One of my favourite phrases in the Bible, 68
On the day of Good Friday, 63
Our Lord spoke these words with utter certainty, 33

Remember me when I am gone away, 51

Since I am coming to that holy room, 64

The death and resurrection of Christ, 74
The faith of Christ teaches more than courage, 62
The Lord is my shepherd, 9
Then I saw a new heaven and a new earth, 69
There is no timetable for the human heart, 32
They are waiting for me, 83
This life is a period of training, 82
Though I speak with the tongues of men, 86

Acknowledgements

The author is very grateful to the following for permission to quote from their works. Every effort has been made to trace the owners of copyright material; the compiler apologises if any inadvertent omission has been made. Information about such omissions should be sent to the publishers who will make full acknowledgement in future editions.

Extracts from the *Book of Common Prayer*, the rights of which are vested in the Crown, are reproduced by permission of the Crown's patentee, Cambridge University Press. Extracts from the New Revised Standard Edition of the Bible, © 1989 by the Division of Christian Education of the National Council of the Churches of Christ in the USA. Used by permission. All rights reserved. *The Alternative Service Book 1980* is copyright © The Central Board of Finance of the Church of England. Extracts are reproduced with permission.

HarperCollins Publishers Ltd.: 'I am not alone' and 'Mourning' from *Plain Prayers for a Complicated World*, Avery Brooke and 'God of the sealed tomb' and 'Now the green blade riseth' from *Easter Garden*, Nicola Slee. The Reverend Giles Harcourt: 'If the great Father Creator'. Mowbray-Cassell plc: 'O Lord Jesus please abide with me' and 'I pray that the true God may protect me tonight' from *Prayers and Thoughts of Chinese Christians*, K K Chan. Collins (Fontana): extracts from *The Resurrection of Christ*, A M Ramsey. The Most Reverend Richard Holloway: 'We are in a garden'. The Right Reverend John Austin: 'It is all grace'. Scottish Academic Press: extracts from Volume 3 of

Carmina Gadelica. Marjorie Pizer, Cremorne, Australia: 'The existence of love' from *Poems for Comfort and Healing*, Pizer, Bookmart Ltd., 1992, originally entitled 'To you the living'. Shoreline Books: 'Joan Mary Fry letter' from *Dust Glorified*, Anne Shells. Darton, Longman and Todd and Templegate Publishers, Springfield, Illinois and Orbis Books, Maryknoll, New York who hold USA rights: extracts from *The Sidelong Glance*, R Holloway; *Letters from the Desert*, Carlo Caretto; *Fire from a Flint*, William Law; *Prayers from a Troubled Heart*, George Appleton; *Gateway to God*, Michael Ramsey; *Through Grief*, Elizabeth Collick and *Landscapes of Glory*, Thomas Traherne. RIB: 'Walking Away' by C Day Lewis. SPCK: 'Love's Constancy' from *Benguine Spirituality*, Fiona Bowie; 'In the midst of life' from *Beyond All Pain*, Ciciley Saunders; 'Christ rising in us' from *The One Genius*, Richard Harries. Macmillan Publisher Ltd.: 'Eden Rock' from *A Field of Vision*, Charles Causley.

The introductions to each section of this book are © Christopher Herbert.

The author acknowledges his indebtedness to the good-humoured forbearance of his secretary, Mrs Kathy Lilley, and to the editorial staff at the National Society for their exemplary help and efficient kindness.

THE NATIONAL SOCIETY

A Christian Voice in Education

The National Society (Church of England) for Promoting Religious Education is a charity which supports all those involved in Christian education – teachers and school governors, students and parents, clergy and lay people – with the resources of its RE centres, archives, courses and conferences.

Founded in 1811, the Society was chiefly responsible for setting up the nationwide network of Church schools in England and Wales and still provides grants for building projects and legal and administrative advice for headteachers and governors. It now publishes a wide range of books, pamphlets and audio-visual items, and two magazines, *Crosscurrent* and *Together*.

For details of membership of the Society or to receive a copy of our current catalogue please contact:

        The Promotions Secretary,
        The National Society,
        Church House,
        Great Smith Street,
        London
        SW1P 3NZ
        Telephone: 071-222 1672